HI! I'M MERIDEE and welcome to **PLANET PLUNK!** Here, you'll learn to play great music while you travel from place to place and chapter to chapter.

PLANET PLUNK

Can't read music? Brand new to piano? No problem! This is the book for you - it uses the power of patterns and fancy-shmancy keyboard diagrams to have you sounding great.

PATTERNS!

DIAGRAMS!

We'll also create, explore, play and have fun, while **earning badges** that will help us pass a final test and zoom along to the next book.

FINGER NUMBERS

THIRDS

IMPROVISE

BUT... I have to warn you. The Villainous C.C. Copycat will probably try to convince you that being creative and exploring are a waste of time. (Her cat Ditto isn't too great either.)

PLUNKADILLO

BWAHAHA!

C.C. comes from a long line of Copycats, who have all been taught to learn music by repeating things and that being creative is UNTHINKABLE.

C.C. took her music lessons from Dr. Blah (my arch-enemy!) himself. Long ago, she tried making her own music. When he laughed at her, she vowed to never do it again.

Do your best to ignore her, and we'll learn, create, play and sound great in no time. Maybe we'll even show her and her students how fun it is to create and explore. Let's get started!

MERIDEE WINTERS SUPER START!
MY FIRST PIANO PATTERNS

Check out a sneak peak of the next book, Chord Quest Level 1!

MERIDEE WINTERS™ SUPER START! MY FIRST PIANO PATTERNS

Meridee Winters Super Start! My First Piano Patterns
© copyright 2005 , 2019 by Meridee Winters. All rights reserved.
Music compositions © copyright 2005, 2019 by Meridee Winters. All right reserved.

Meridee Winters Publishing • 63 W. Lancaster Ave., Suite 7 • Ardmore, PA 19003
www.MerideeWintersMusicMethod.com
ISBN: 978-1-943821-52-5
Meridee Winters: Music Composer, Author, and Art Director
Kate Capps: Editor, Creative Consultant
Madé Dimas Wirawan: Character Design and Illustrations
Armand Alidio: Cover Design, Additional Illustrations
Krysta Bernhardt: Layout, Graphic Design, Additional Illustrations
Sean Miller: Additional Illustrations
Gabriel Rhopers: Creative Consultant; Kaitlin Borden, Peter Horst: Proofreading

Connect With Us at
merideewintersmusicmethod.com

Your first destination is the Launch Pad. Here, you'll learn the basics about your hands and the keyboard. Then you'll use that knowledge to play your way around Planet Plunk!

We'll also keep an eye on what's happening on Planet Blah. Currently, C.C. Copycat is teaching music in her typical Copycat style.

SPACE STORM

You've landed on Planet Plunk during a storm! Create a musical storm by improvising all over the keyboard. Revisit this exercise again and again as you become more familiar with the piano!

1 Storm Fingers

Try playing the piano these ways:

● Raindrops - tiny high twinkly notes

● Lightning - sharp crashes or groups of notes

● Far away thunder - low slow groups of notes

● Close Thunder - low and loud

● Combine into a storm - play wildly all over!

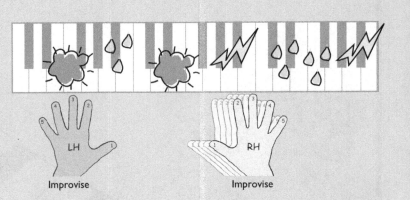

2 Fingerpaint your storm

Now combine the different ways to play into your own improvisation!

Play high twinkly notes

Squish some low notes.

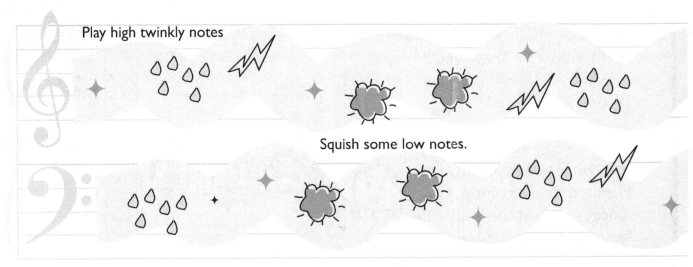

3 Play 4 ways

Make it a game! Get your creativity flowing by alternating these different ways to play.

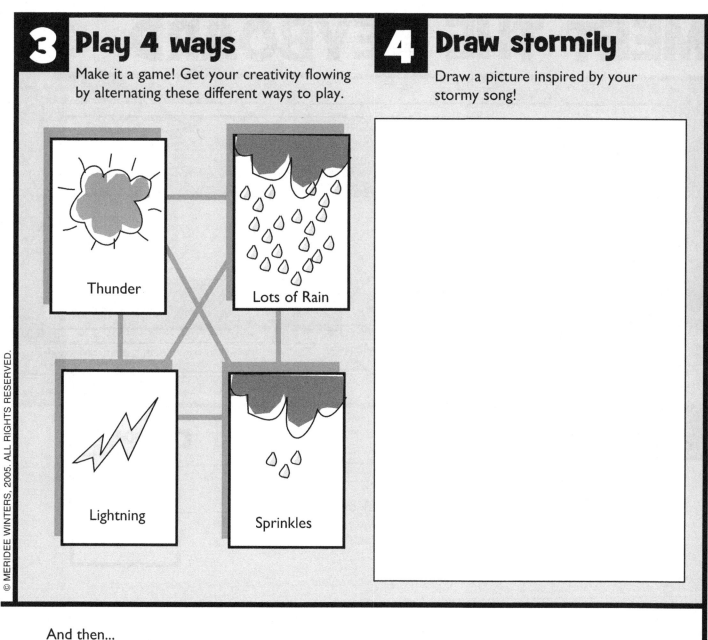

4 Draw stormily

Draw a picture inspired by your stormy song!

And then...

And then...

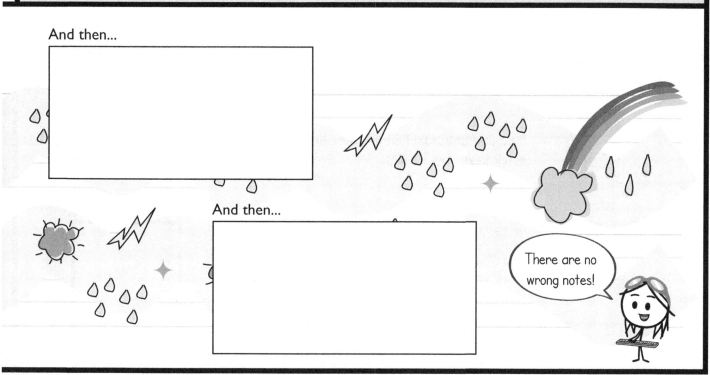

There are no wrong notes!

MEET THE KEYBOARD

The keyboard has black keys and white keys, going low (left) to high (right). Let's take a tour!

1 White Keys

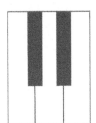

Find the lowest white key on the piano. Play all the white keys low to high.

2 Black Keys

Find and SMOOSH all the sets of 2 black keys, low to high.

Start high and SMOOSH all the set of 3 black keys, high to low.

MERIDEE WINTERS SUPER START! MY FIRST PIANO PATTERNS

KEY EXPLORER

EXPLORE

Prove your key skills by completing each challenge on the stars below!

Play all of the sets of two black keys from low to high and then high to low.

Play some high white keys. Play softly and quickly. Tiptoe!

Play a set of 3 low black keys loudly, then softly.

Play some low white keys. Play slowly and loudly. Stomp!

Play a set of 2 black keys softly and quickly.

Play all of the sets of 3 black keys low to high and then high to low.

Play any keys you want.

What animals do the high keys sound like? The low keys?

FINGERPAINT WITH BLACK KEYS

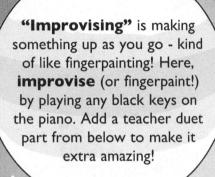

"**Improvising**" is making something up as you go - kind of like fingerpainting! Here, **improvise** (or fingerpaint!) by playing any black keys on the piano. Add a teacher duet part from below to make it extra amazing!

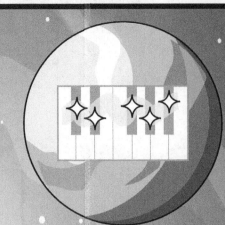

Explore with black keys

Keep playing

Get into the flow

Teacher/Student Duets

Jazzy Jam

Penta Jam

Tip! This part has a descending bass line, and the top notes stay the same for almost all of it!

Tip! Keep the pedal down and play peacefully. The five black keys form a pentatonic scale, which has its roots in the Far East.

Teachers: For bright, colorful versions of these activities (and more games!) use a MW teacher gamebook.

FINGERPAINT WITH WHITE KEYS

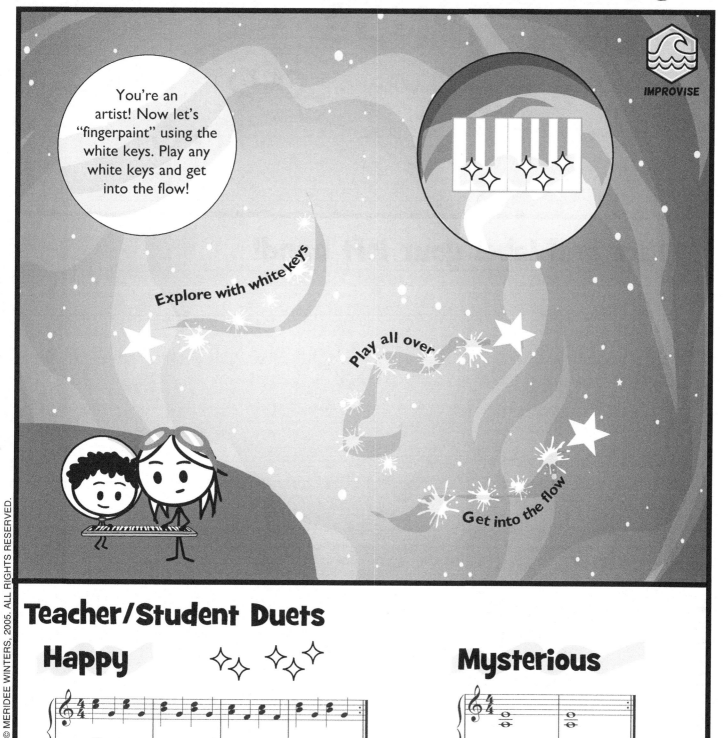

You're an artist! Now let's "fingerpaint" using the white keys. Play any white keys and get into the flow!

IMPROVISE

Explore with white keys

Play all over

Get into the flow

Teacher/Student Duets

Happy

Play at a medium tempo.

Mysterious

Play at a slow mysterious tempo.

Teachers: For bright, colorful versions of these activities (and more games!) use a MW teacher gamebook.

YOUR HANDS

Your hands and fingers allow you to make great music. Learning the number of each finger lets you know which one to play.

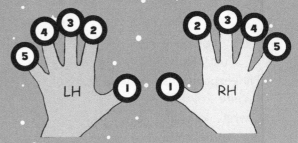

Trace and label your left hand!

LEFT HAND

MERIDEE WINTERS SUPER START! MY FIRST PIANO PATTERNS

Finger Fun One at a time, place each finger on the number where it belongs.

LH

RH

Trace and label your right hand!

RIGHT HAND

MY FIRST PATTERN PIECE: STAR CLIMBER

Now that you know finger numbers and have explored the keyboard, you're ready for your first pattern song! This song only uses two fingers, but sounds amazing!

I How to Play

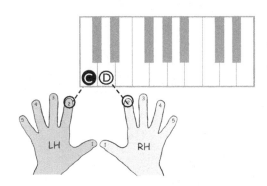

Play C with your left hand finger 2. Then Play D (the note next to it) with your right hand finger 2.

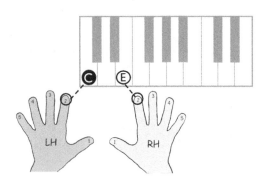

Your left hand stays put! Play C with left hand finger 2 again. Move your right hand up another note and play E with finger 2.

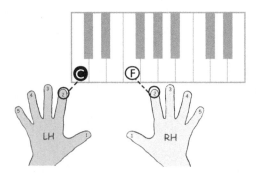

Your left hand still stays put! Play C with left hand finger 2 again. Move your right hand up one note to play F with finger 2. Repeat this left-right pattern until your right hand reaches C!

2 Play the pattern

- With your hands in position (LH on C, RH on D), get ready to play the pattern.

- Your hands will take turns: left (C), right (D), left (C), right (E), etc.

- Can you name the notes as you play?

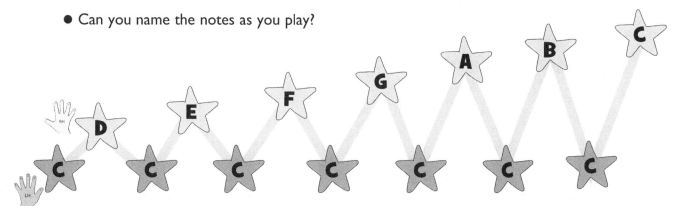

 Now reverse it! Try playing this pattern from a higher C moving DOWN. (C B C A C G C F C E, etc.)

3 You're an adventurer!

Play the song all the way through each of these five ways.

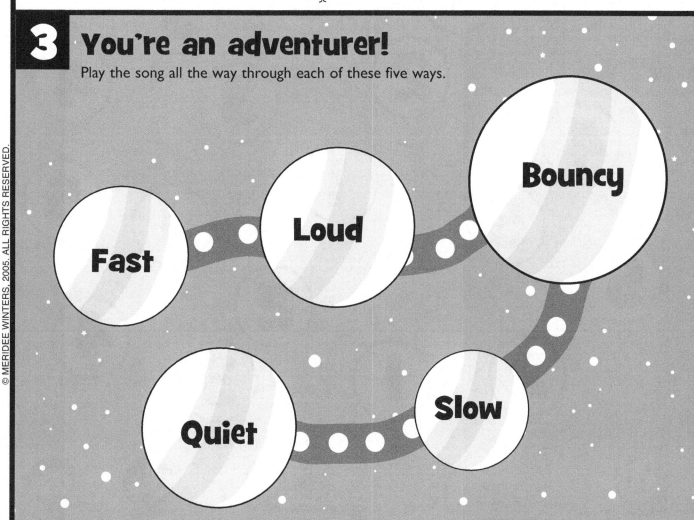

Fast

Loud

Bouncy

Quiet

Slow

QUANTUM QUIZ!

1 Label the finger numbers

2 Finger Flash!

1. With your right hand, play the game by touching each circle with the correct finger number.
2. Repeat the game with your left hand. (For an extra challenge, time yourself.)

You did it! You earned these powers and are ready to learn more!

FINGER NUMBERS   IMPROVISE   EXPLORE

Chapter 2

BLACK KEYS

You completed your training at the launch pad! Now you get to travel to one of Planet Plunk's top vacation spots: The Black Keys!

The word "keys" can mean different things, like keys to a door or piano keys (of course!). But did you know that "keys" can also be a series of islands?

Slap on some supersolar sunscreen and let's visit the Black Keys!

DRAGONFLUTTERS
Two Black Keys

Wings flutter as we explore high and low. In this exercise we will play all the groups of two black keys. To warm up, try fluttering your fingers in the air or on your leg!

1 Circle the groups of two black keys

Find and circle the groups of two black keys below.

BLACK KEYS

Low ←   High →

2 Play with right hand "wings"

Place RH fingers 2 and 3 on the lowest group of two black keys. Using your "wings," play the exercise, moving up one group at a time.

Keep going to the top, then turn around and go back down the keyboard. Flutter about!

Here is a pattern! Try it up and down the keyboard!

3 Play with left hand "wings"

Place LH fingers 3 and 2 on the lowest group of two black keys. Using your "wings," play the exercise, moving up one group at a time.

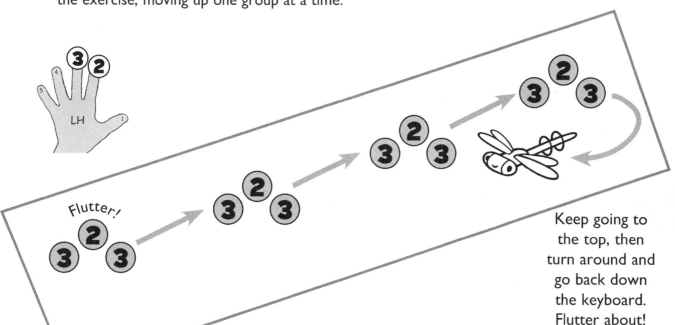

Keep going to the top, then turn around and go back down the keyboard. Flutter about!

4 Explore!

Try playing the sets of two black keys these different ways:

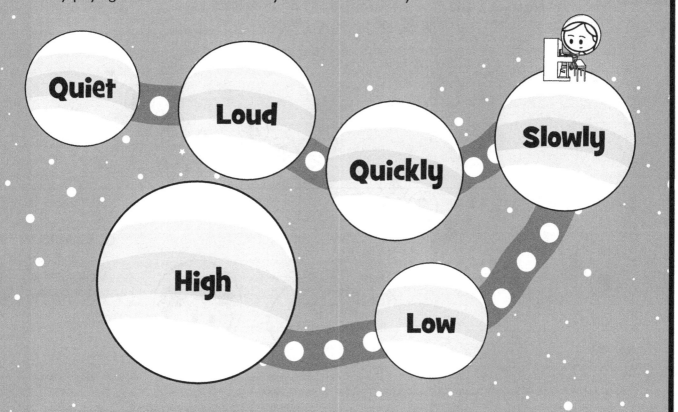

ASTRO ANTS
Three Black Keys

Ants march steadily as they explore high and low. In this exercise we will play all the groups of three black keys. To warm up, try marching your ant fingers anywhere!

1 Circle groups of three black keys

Find and circle the groups of three black keys below.

BLACK KEYS

Low   High

2 March with right hand

Place RH fingers 2, 3 and 4 on the lowest group of three black keys. Then play each key, marching up one group at a time.

Here is a pattern! Try it up and down the keyboard!

Go to the top of the piano, turn around and go back down.

3 March with left hand

Place LH fingers 4, 3 and 2 on the lowest group of three black keys.
Then play each key, marching up one group at a time.

4 3 2 — LH

March!
4 3 2 → **4 3 2** → **4 3 2** → **4 3 2** → **4 3 2**

Go to the top,
turn around and
go back down.
March about!

4 Explore!

Try playing the sets of three black keys these different ways:

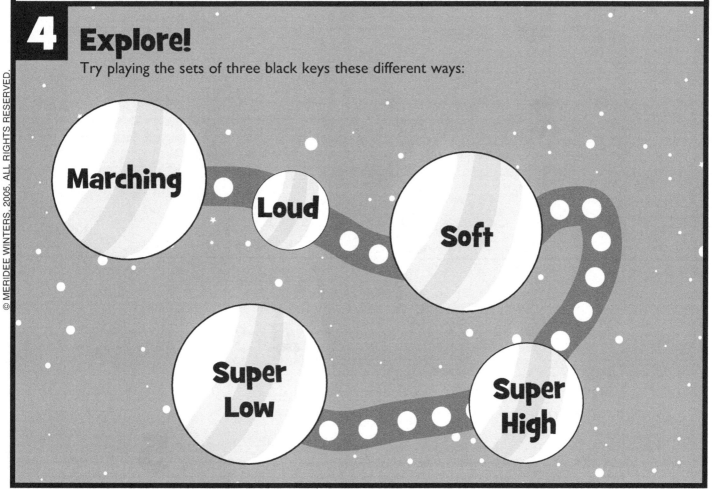

Marching

Loud

Soft

Super Low

Super High

MARY HAD A LITTLE LAMB

On the black keys

Using the set of three black keys and fingers 2,3 and 4, you can play this famous song!

Play each finger one at a time

• On a set of three black keys, play the farthest black key to the right with RH finger 4.

• Then use RH finger number 3 to play the next note (the middle black key).

• Then use finger number 2 to play the left black key.

• Play the finger numbers on the next page to play the full song.

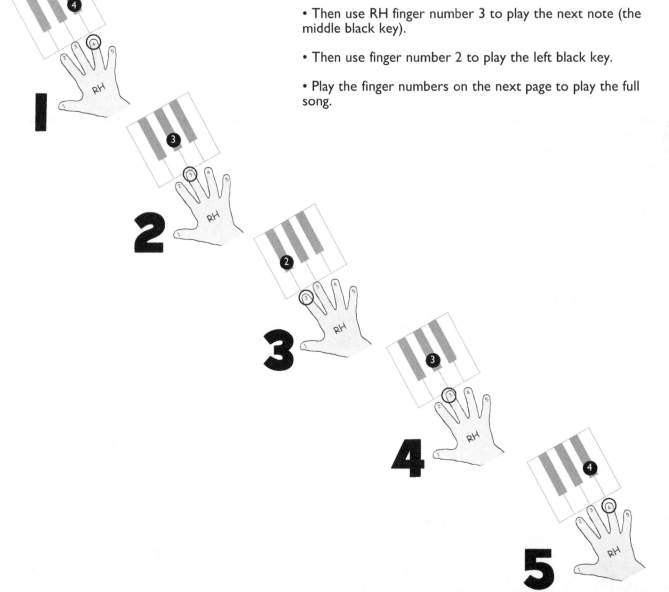

MARY HAD A LITTLE LAMB

This familar tune uses the skills you just learned to play a real song! For more classic songs, check out the book "Meridee Winters Easy Piano Songs for Kids!"

BAAAAAAA!

④ ③ ② ③ ④ ④ ④

Ma-ry had a lit-tle lamb,

③ ③ ③ ④ ④ ④

lit-tle lamb, lit-tle lamb,

④ ③ ② ③ ④ ④ ④

Ma-ry had a lit-tle lamb

④ ③ ③ ④ ③ ②

whose fleece was white as snow!

PARODY TIME!

A parody is when you write new (usually funny!) words to a song. Try our lyrics and then write your own!

Alternate lyrics!

Mary had a lunar lamb, lunar lamb, lunar lamb
Mary had a lunar lamb who lived upon the moon
He was in a lunar band, lunar band, lunar band
He was in a lunar band – he played the bassoon!

Write your own parody by writing new lyrics to "Mary Had a Little Lamb":

Mary had a _____
_____
_____
_____

QUANTUM QUIZ!

1 **Smoosh.** Smoosh all the sets of black keys on the piano.

2 **Perform!** Play "Mary Had a Little Lamb" on the black keys for family or friends.

3 **Finger Flashback!** Let's drill finger numbers again so we're super prepared for our adventure in the next chapter. Press each circle with the correct finger on your right hand. Then repeat with your left hand.

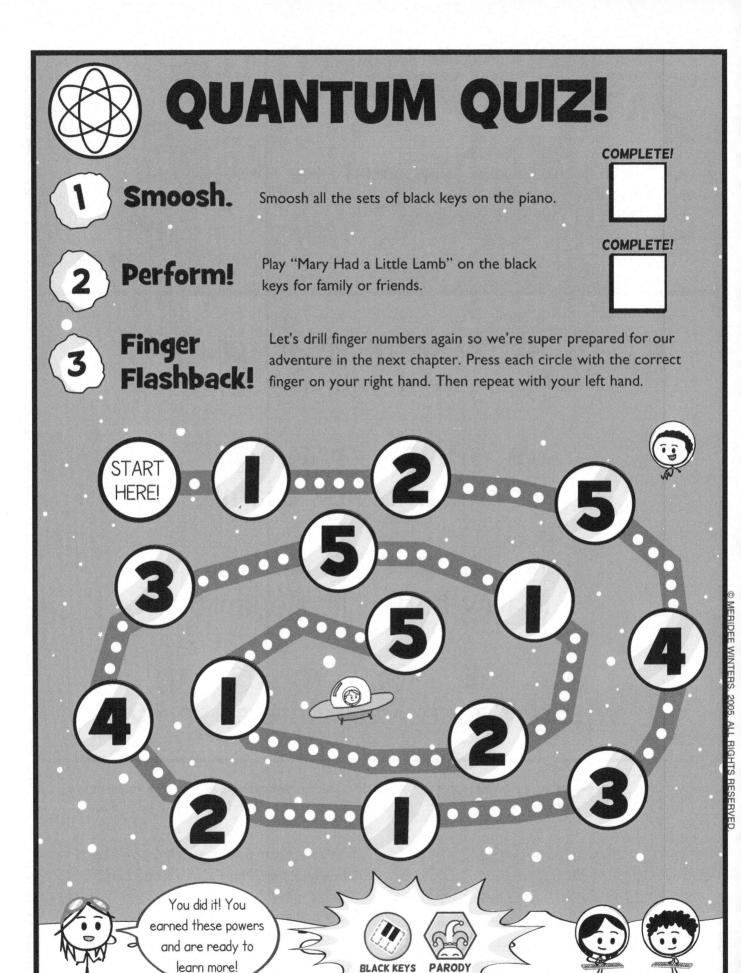

You did it! You earned these powers and are ready to learn more!

BLACK KEYS   PARODY

You've successfuly navigated the Black Keys! Now let's fly on over to another set of lovely Plunk Islands: The White Keys. Let's explore!

WHITE KEYS

Now we will learn the names of the white keys. Each of the seven white keys has a name that comes from the musical alphabet. Using the groups of black keys as markers can help find the notes.

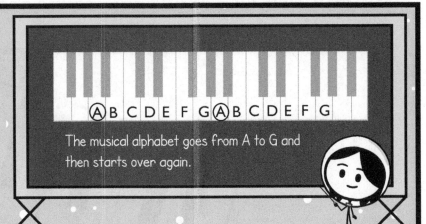

The musical alphabet goes from A to G and then starts over again.

1 Musical Alphabet

Finish filling in the musical alphabet on the keyboard below.

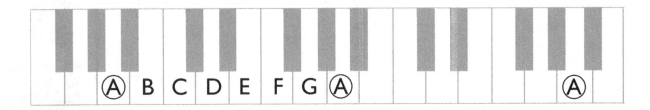

2 Circle, label and play

Start by labeling each A and then fill in the rest of the keyboards below.   Start at the bottom of your piano keyboard and play and say each note all the way up!

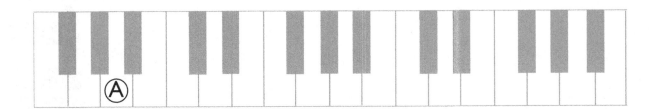

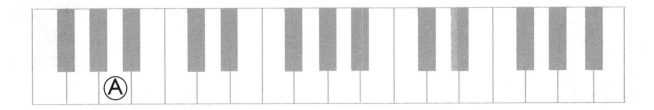

PLUNK PARADE

DUET PART

 Tip! Now that you know D and A, you can revisit the Black Key Fingerpainting exercise on page 6 and add those two notes – Fingerpaint with the Black Keys PLUS D & A and hear the magical results!

WHITE KEYS

MOONBEAM TOCCATA

This dramatic song is a favorite at Meridee's school, and is similar to the Star Climber song from Chapter 1. For some added mystery, try holding the pedal down through the whole song.

1 Place hands

● Put your LH finger 2 on A. Keep it there the entire time

● Put your RH finger 2 on B, but be ready to move it around.

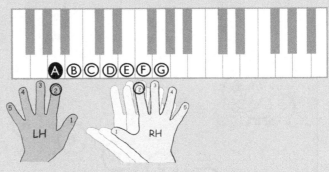

play one at a time

2 Play the pattern

● With your hands in position, LH on A, RH on B, get ready to play the pattern.

● Your hands will take turns: left (A), right (B), left (A), right (C), etc.

● Can you name the notes as you play?

LISTEN! Listen to Toccata and Fugue in D Minor by J.S. Bach for another dramatic toccata!

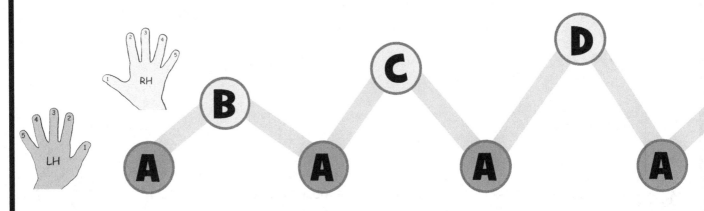

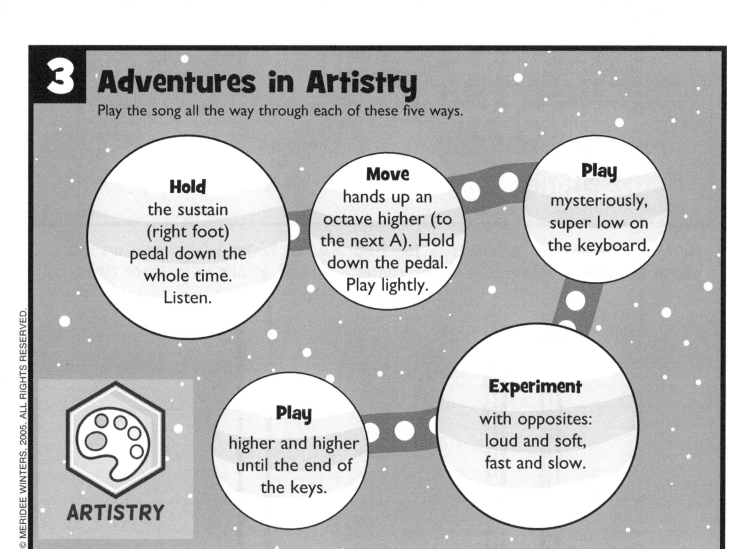

3 Adventures in Artistry

Play the song all the way through each of these five ways.

Hold the sustain (right foot) pedal down the whole time. Listen.

Move hands up an octave higher (to the next A). Hold down the pedal. Play lightly.

Play mysteriously, super low on the keyboard.

Play higher and higher until the end of the keys.

Experiment with opposites: loud and soft, fast and slow.

ARTISTRY

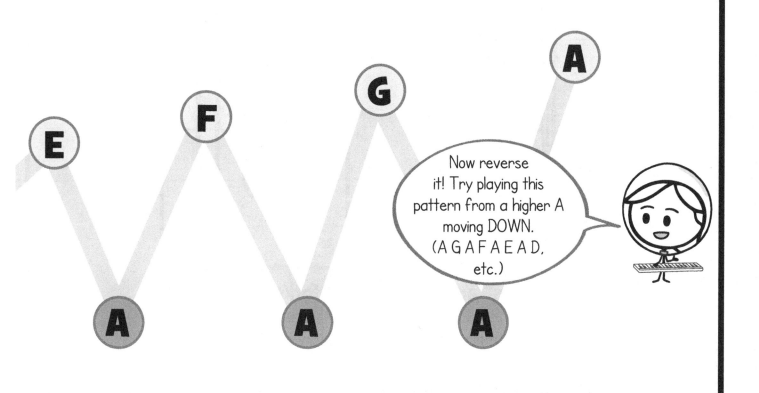

Now reverse it! Try playing this pattern from a higher A moving DOWN. (A G A F A E A D, etc.)

SECRET TRICK
for remembering the piano keys

Here's a super start secret trick for figuring out which white keys on the piano are which. Imagine a set of chopsticks and a fork with three tines:

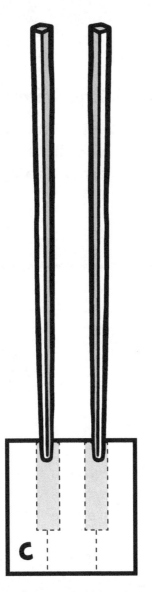

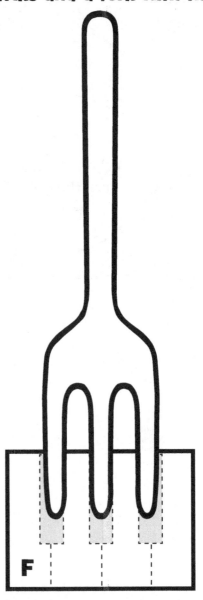

The "Chopsticks" are the sets of two black keys.
The key to the left of the "chopsticks" is C. (Think: "C is for Chopsticks!")

The "forks" are the sets of three black keys.
The key to the left of the "fork" is F. (Think: "F is for Fork!")

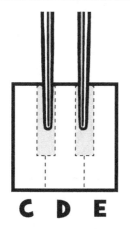

Use the "C is for Chopsticks" trick to find D and E.

Find C, then play the next note to its right. That's D.
The next note is E!

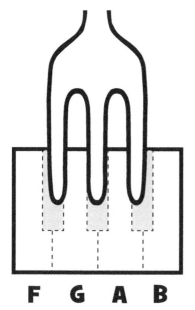

Use the "F is for Fork" trick to find G, A and B.

Find F, then play the next note to its right. That's G.
The next note is A. The note after that is B.

FILL IN THE LETTERS BELOW.

Next let's practice finding and playing these groups of keys!

C, D & E

Now let's take a closer look at the white keys that are grouped around the two black keys.

---

1 Circle, label and play: C

C is to the left of the two black keys. Circle the groups of two black keys. Then label and play all the C's on the keyboard.

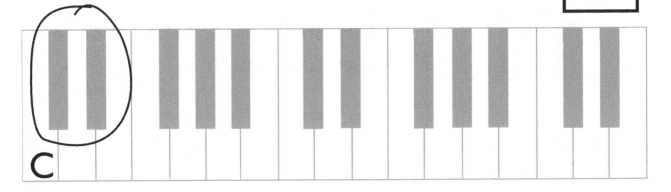

C

---

2 Circle, label and play: D

D is in the middle of the two black keys. Circle all the groups of two black keys. Then label and play all the D's on the keyboard

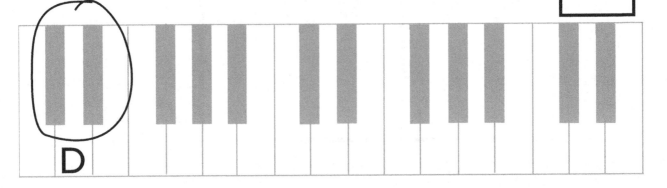

D

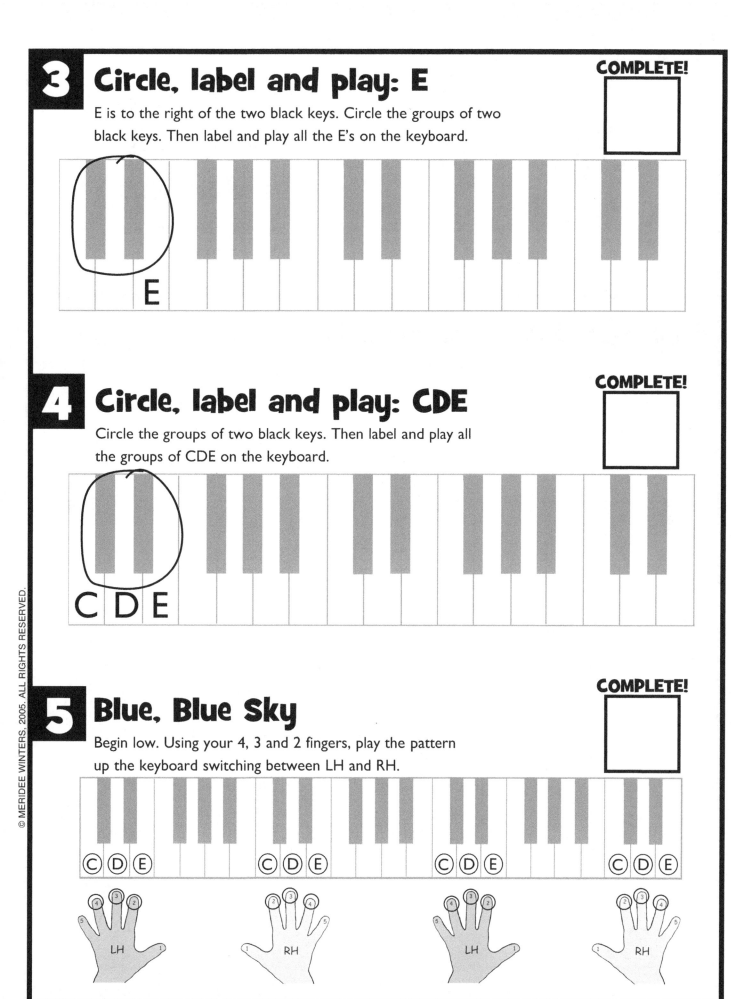

3 Circle, label and play: E

E is to the right of the two black keys. Circle the groups of two black keys. Then label and play all the E's on the keyboard.

E

4 Circle, label and play: CDE

Circle the groups of two black keys. Then label and play all the groups of CDE on the keyboard.

C D E

5 Blue, Blue Sky

Begin low. Using your 4, 3 and 2 fingers, play the pattern up the keyboard switching between LH and RH.

C D E   C D E   C D E   C D E

LH   RH   LH   RH

MARY HAD A LITTLE LAMB

On the white keys

Now you can play this iconic song on the white keys!

Play each finger one at a time

- Play E with RH finger 4.

- Then use RH finger number 3 to play D.

- Then use finger number 2 to play C.

- Play the finger numbers on the next page to play the full song.

1

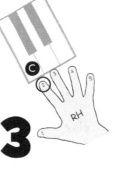

2

3

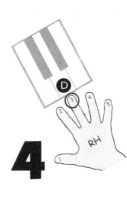

4

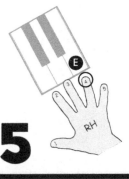

5

MARY HAD A LITTLE LAMB

This song is an excerpt from the "Meridee Winters Easy Piano Songs for Kids" book! Check it out for even more classic favorites!

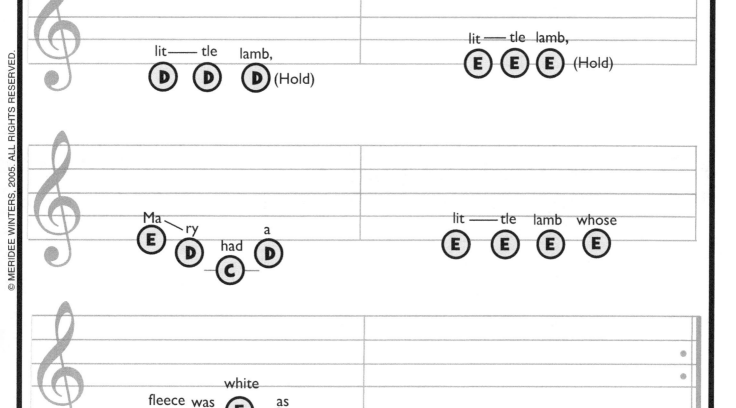

F, G, A & B

Now we'll take a closer look at the white keys that are grouped around the three black keys.

1 ## Circle, label and play: F F is to the left of the three black keys - just after E. Circle all the groups of three black keys. Then label and play all the F's on the keyboard.

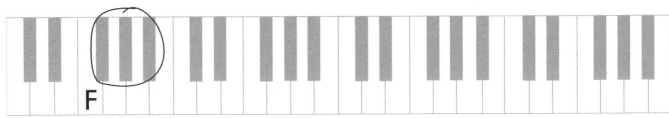

F

2 ## Circle, label and play: G G is in the middle of the three black keys - just after F. Circle all the groups of three black keys. Then label and play all the G's on the keyboard.

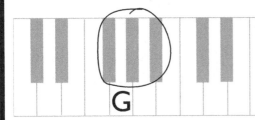

G

MERIDEE WINTERS SUPER START! MY FIRST PIANO PATTERNS

3 Circle, label and play: A

A is in the middle of the three black keys - just after G. Circle all the groups of three black keys. Then label and play all the A's on the keyboard.

COMPLETE!

A

4 Circle, label and play: B

B is to the right of the three black keys - just after A. Circle all the groups of three black keys. Then label and play all the B's on the keyboard.

COMPLETE!

B

5 Deep, Dark Sea

COMPLETE!

Begin low. Using your 1, 2, 3 and 4 fingers, play the pattern up the keyboard, switching between LH and RH.

F G A B   F G A B   F G A B   F G A B

LH   RH   LH   RH

QUANTUM QUIZ!

Key Quest: Pass your quiz by completing the game below. Point to a meteor. Say and play the note on the piano or follow the instructions on that meteor. Try moving in different directions and revisit this exercise every lesson to build your note finding skills. For more great skill-building games, check out a Meridee Winters Game Book!

MERIDEE WINTERS SUPER START! MY FIRST PIANO PATTERNS

Chapter

4

PATTERN LAUNCH

Now that you've explored all over the keys, you're ready to head to the Plunk Peaks - a musical mountain range of patterns going up and down!

So much of music is just patterns combined in different (beautiful) ways. By learning patterns, we can play great sounding songs right away - even if we can't read music yet. Let's try it. Onward and upward!

BLAH-VISION

MEANWHILE ON PLANET BLAH...

Sorry, kiddos: no interesting songs until you can read music. Remember: the wait is long to play good songs.

MYSTERIOUS MOUNTAIN

1 Place hands and practice the pattern

- First, practice bouncing your fingers on the closed lid of the piano.

- Pretend you are bouncing a ball. Say "left, left, right, right" and keep a steady beat.

- Now, place LH finger 2 on A and play. Repeat.

- Place RH finger 2 on B and play. Repeat.

- Repeat the pattern, keeping your LH finger 2 on A, but climbing your RH up the keyboard one note at a time.

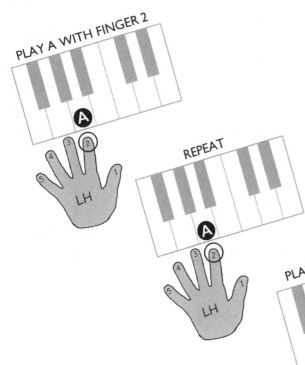

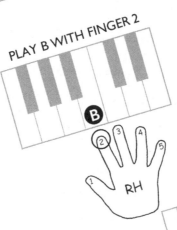

2 Play the pattern

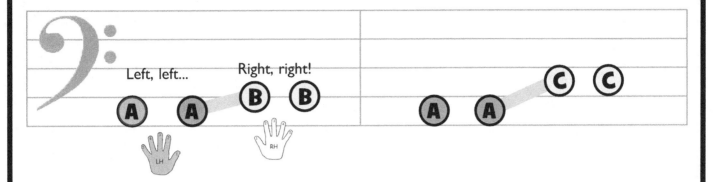

Left, left... Right, right!
Ⓐ Ⓐ Ⓑ Ⓑ   Ⓐ Ⓐ Ⓒ Ⓒ

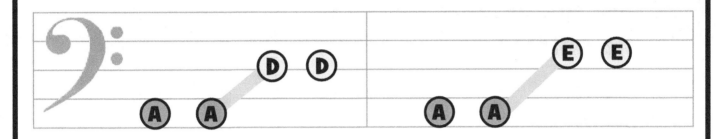

Ⓐ Ⓐ Ⓓ Ⓓ   Ⓐ Ⓐ Ⓔ Ⓔ

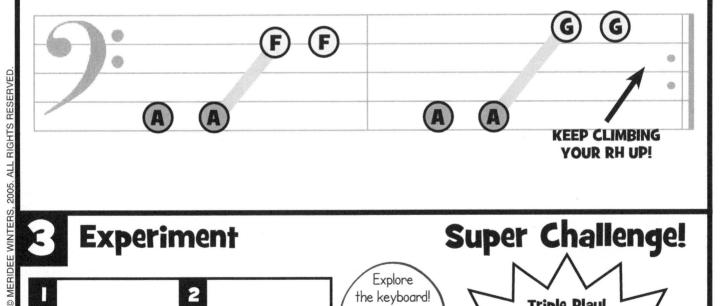

Ⓐ Ⓐ Ⓕ Ⓕ   Ⓐ Ⓐ Ⓖ Ⓖ

KEEP CLIMBING
YOUR RH UP!

3 Experiment

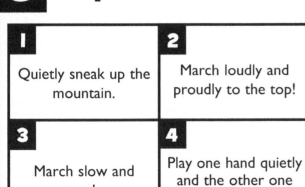

1	**2**
Quietly sneak up the mountain.	March loudly and proudly to the top!

3	**4**
March slow and steady.	Play one hand quietly and the other one LOUDLY!

Explore the keyboard! What new worlds will you discover?

Super Challenge!

Triple Play!
Can you play each note 3 times in a row instead of two?
Left, two, three, Right, two, three...
Make your own challenge!

MOUNTAIN MELODY

I Plce hands and practice the pattern

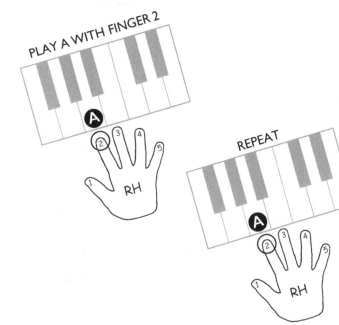

PLAY A WITH FINGER 2

REPEAT

Keep your RH on the same note for the whole exercise!

* First, practice bouncing your fingers on the closed lid of the piano.

* Pretend you are bouncing a ball. Say "right, right, left, left" and keep a steady beat.

* Now, place RH finger 2 on A and play. Repeat.

* Place LH finger 2 on G and play. Repeat.

* Repeat the pattern, keeping you RH finger 2 on A, but climbing your LH down the keyboard one note at a time.

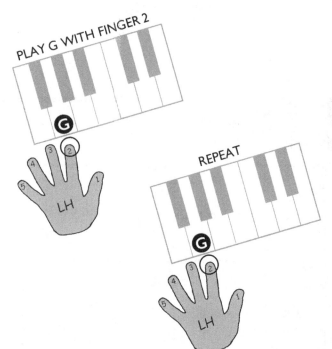

PLAY G WITH FINGER 2

REPEAT

MERIDEE WINTERS SUPER START! MY FIRST PIANO PATTERNS

2 Play the pattern

Right, right... left, left!

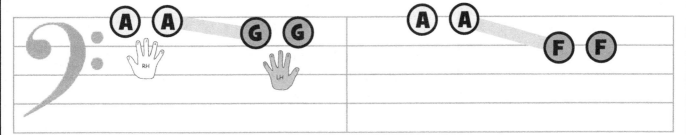

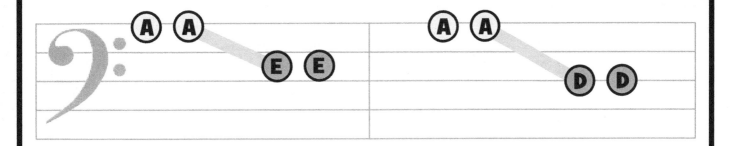

KEEP CLIMBING YOUR LH DOWN!

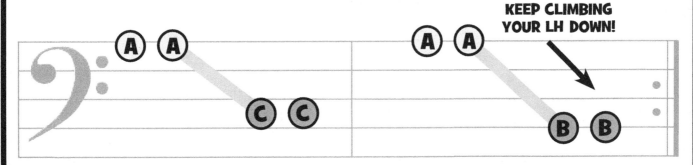

3 Explore

Super Challenge!

1 "Tiptoe" down the notes.	**2** "Stomp" down the keyboard as you play!
3 Play it super low.	**4** Play one hand quietly and the other one LOUDLY!

Explore the song! Music is an adventure!

Triple Play!
Can you play each note 3 times in a row instead of two?
Right, two, three...
Left, two, three...
Make your own challenge!

COSMIC BLUES

1 Practice the LH Bass line

 =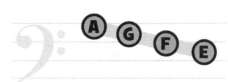

Practice until smooth!

2 Play with both hands

- Place LH finger 1 on A and play.
- Place your RH 1 finger on the A an octave higher and play.
- Then play G with your LH finger 2.
- Play the RH A again.
- Play F with LH finger 3.
- Play the RH A again.
- Play E with LH finger 4.
- Play the RH A again.

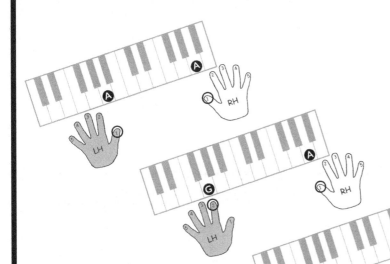

 LISTEN! Listen to "Stray Cat Strut" by the Stray Cats. Can you hear this pattern?

THE BLUES

3 Play the pattern

Right!
(A)
RH

Left...
(A) ——————— (G)

(A)   (A)

KEEP REPEATING THE PATTERN!

(F) ——————— (E)

4 PERFORM!

Perform this blues song for family or friends. Try the options below to make it shine.

PERFORMANCE

1 Make "tickets" for your performance.

2 Make up words.

Write lyrics or draw a picture of your performance!

3 Move your head to the beat.

4 Ask the audience to snap their fingers to the beat.

QUANTUM QUIZ!

1 **Play.** Play Mysterious Mountain. BONUS: Can you play it from memory?

COMPLETE!

2 **Pattern Plunkifier!** Pick a hand. Choose a finger number pattern from the planets below on the left, and combine with a starting note from the right to experiment with different patterns. Then diverge and improvise to come up with more patterns or even a full song!

COMPLETE!

Create Your Own!

Congrats! You played your first patterns and earned more powers. Next, you will laser focus on patterns that use neighbor notes, also called "seconds."

PERFORMANCE

THE BLUES

We've made it to Planet Plunk's biggest desert—
the Supersonic Sand Dunes! Here's we'll learn
about intervals, specifically seconds.

Intervals refer to space. Not outer space, but
the space between two notes – we call that an
interval. In this chapter, we'll learn about the
interval of a second. Seconds are neighbor
notes. A friendly place to start!

INTERVALS: SECONDS

Chapter
5

SECONDS: NEIGHBORS

Seconds are sometimes called neighbor notes because they are right next to each other, only a step apart. In this exercise, you will play seconds one at a time and together.

Play each finger one at a time

SECONDS

- Start with finger 1 (thumb) on C.
- C is the note to the left of two black keys.
- Then use finger number 2 to play the next note, D.
- Now play them together.

Play finger 1

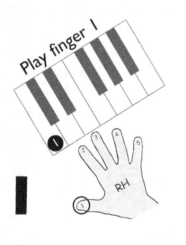

1

Play finger 2

2

Play both together

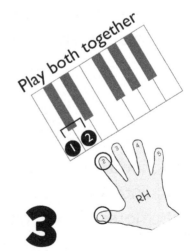

3

Neighbor notes are called 2nds!

Now move up a key and repeat!

DESERT BLOBS

Step, step, squish! Step, step, squish!
It's time to use our neighbors and squish up
the keyboard. Remember: keep it squishy,
steady and even.

For a "three note squish" version of this
song, visit mwfunstuff.com/superstart

Step, step,
squish, up!
Step, step,
squish, up!

SAND SHARKS

Swim with these seconds if you dare! Play super low on the keyboard.

DUET! Teachers or parents, try playing a droning E minor chord as the student plays.

Da Dum (B)(C) Da Dum (B)(C)   (C)(D) (C)(D)

(D)(E) (D)(E)   (E)(F) (E)(F)

(F)(G) (F)(G)   (G)(A) (G)(A)

(A)(B) (A)(B)   (B)(C)— (B)(C)—

REPEAT

LISTEN! Listen to the theme from "Jaws" for another suspenseful seconds tune!

PLUNKADILLO POLKA

Now use a similar second pattern with your right hand, going up!

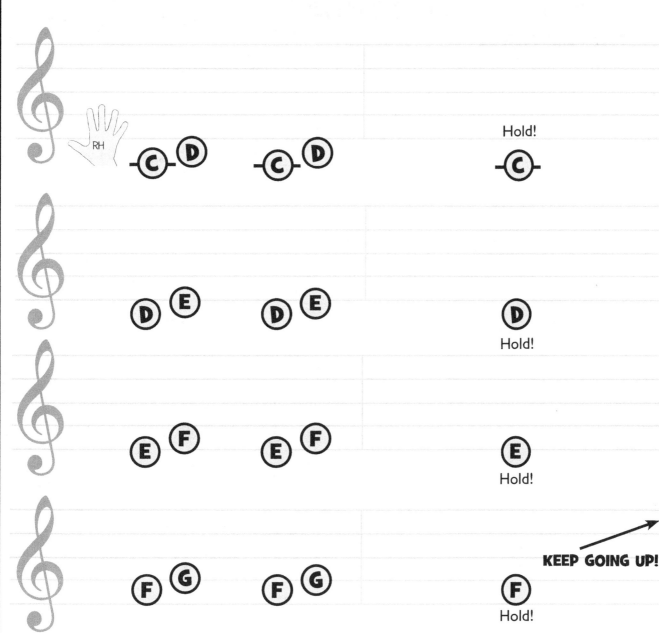

STRUMBLEWEED

Place hands and practice the pattern

● Place LH finger 1 on C and play.

● Answer by playing D and then E with RH fingers 1 and 2.

● Keeping your LH on C, move your RH up one note and play E and F.

● Keep climbing your RH up the keyboard one note at a time.

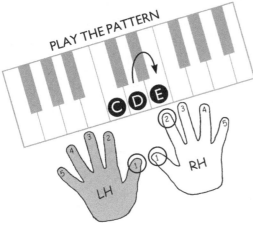

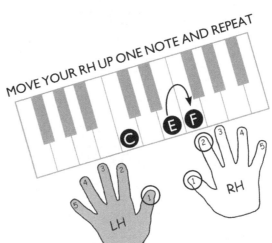

KEEP CLIMBING UP!

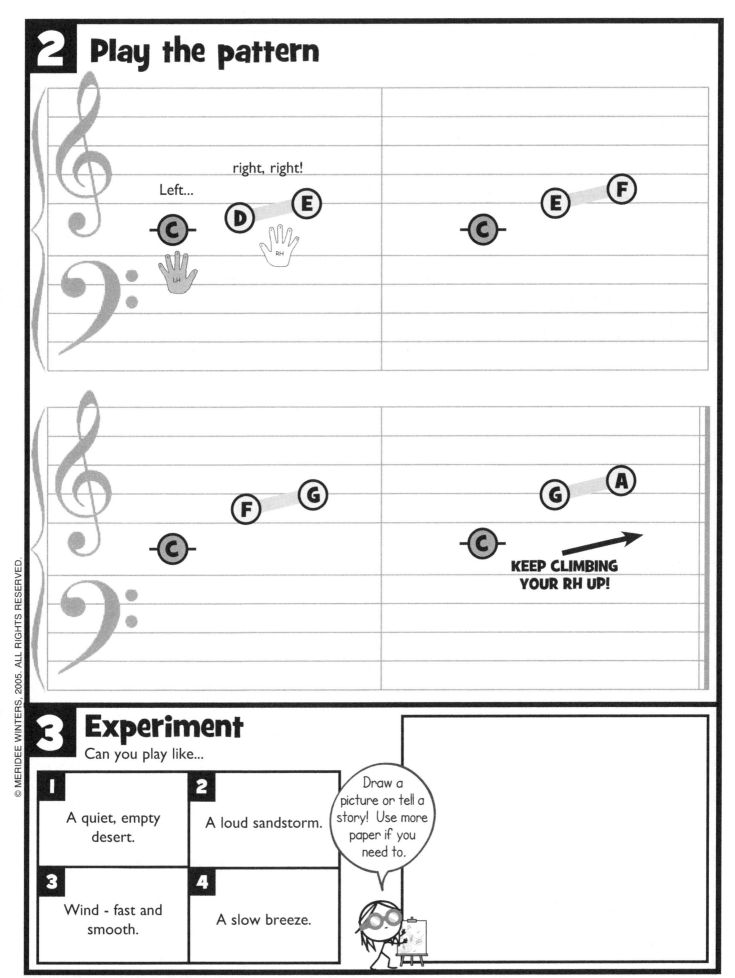

DESERT FOOTSTEPS

1. Place hands and practice the pattern

- Place LH finger 1 on A and play.

- Answer by playing B and then C with RH fingers 1 and 2.

- Keeping your LH on A, move your RH up one note and play C and D.

- Keep climbing your RH up the keyboard one note at a time.

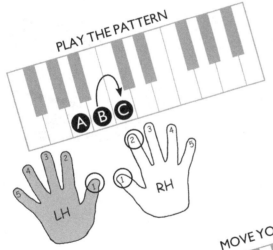

KEEP CLIMBING UP!

LISTEN! Listen to "In the Hall of the Mountain King" by Grieg for a song with a similar mood.

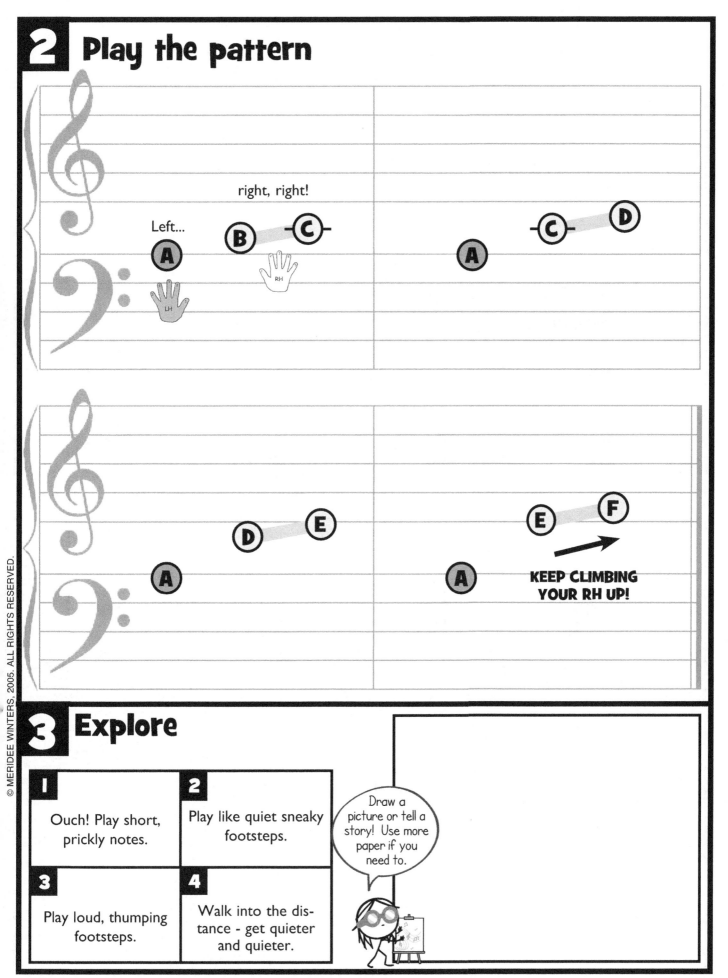

QUANTUM QUIZ!

 1 Knowledge. Seconds are sometimes called _____, because they are right next to each other.

A) Buddy notes
B) Sibling notes
C) Neighbor notes

 2 Seconds Supernova! Play a second starting on each note below. (For example, for C, you'll play C and D to make a second.)

 E   C   B   E

G   A   F   C

 3 Perform! Play "Desert Footsteps" for family or friends.

 Congrats! You've learned about seconds and earned these powers. Now you're ready to learn another interval: thirds!

SECONDS   LISTENING

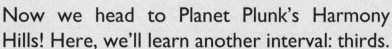

Chapter 6

INTERVALS: THIRDS

Now we head to Planet Plunk's Harmony Hills! Here, we'll learn another interval: thirds.

This harmonious interval is one step bigger than a second. The third is the note that decides if that moment in the music sounds happy or sad. Let's play thirds!

HILLTOP MYSTERY

These hills are full of mystery! What does this tune make you imagine?

1 How to Play

- Put your RH finger 1 (thumb) on C and play.

- Skip a note and play E with finger 3.

- Now play them together!

- Play them together another time!

THIRDS

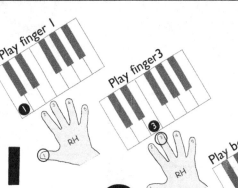

1

2

3

4

2 Practice

Using your 1 and 3 fingers, practice playing thirds one at a time, then together.

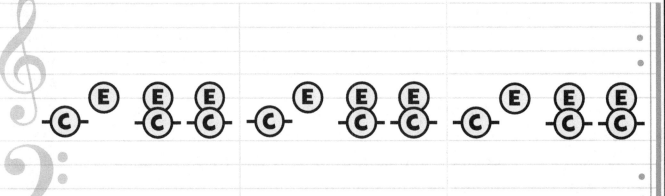

2 Play the pattern

Play the pattern from the previous page, but start on D. Notice how that changes the mood!

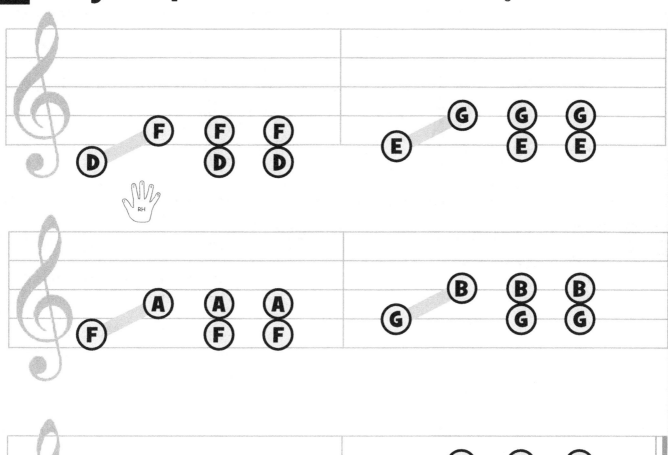

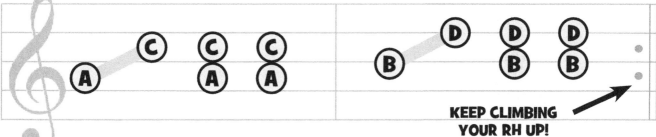

KEEP CLIMBING YOUR RH UP!

3 Experiment

Can you play these ways?

1 Play like wind in the hills – quiet and smooth.

2 Play like you're marching up a hill.

3 Play slowly and mysteriously.

4 Duet! Teacher plays steady LH beat with low D.

Try playing this song with a drum.

FLICKERING FIREFLIES

1 Place hands and practice the pattern

- With your LH finger 1, play an F.

- Answer by playing G and B together two times with RH fingers 1 and 3.

- Keep your LH on F, but move your RH up one note. Play A and C together two times.

- Keep climbing your RH up the keyboard one note at a time, repeating the pattern.

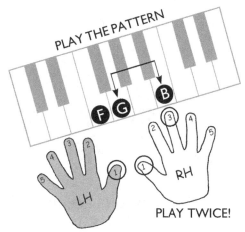

PLAY THE PATTERN

PLAY TWICE!

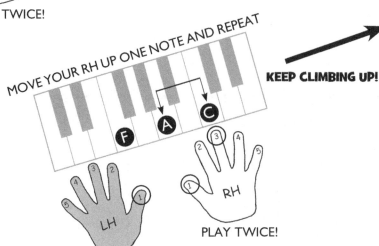

MOVE YOUR RH UP ONE NOTE AND REPEAT

KEEP CLIMBING UP!

PLAY TWICE!

Keep your LH on the same note for the whole exercise!

LISTEN! Listen to the theme from the Pixar movie "Up." Can you hear this pattern?

2 Play the pattern

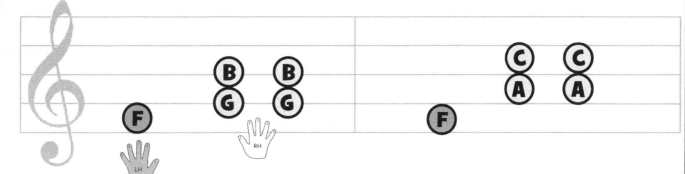

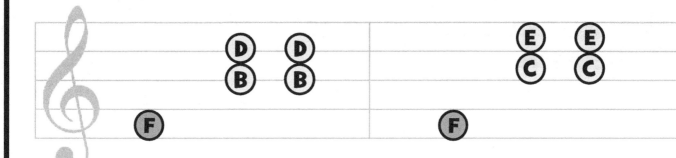

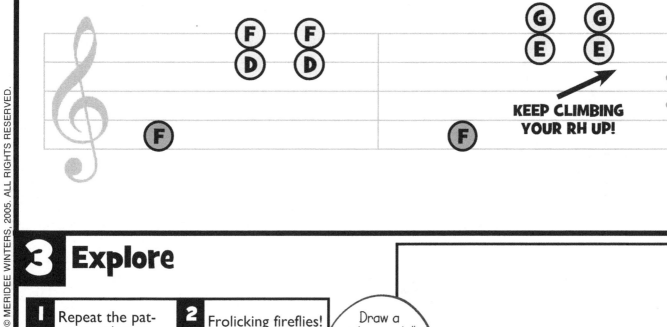

KEEP CLIMBING YOUR RH UP!

3 Explore

1 Repeat the pattern going up then down, up then down, hill after hill.

2 Frolicking fireflies! Make the notes sound quick and bouncy.

3 Try playing starting on C or A instead of F. How does the mood change?

4 What do you see or imagine is happening? Make a story.

Draw a picture or tell a story! Use more paper if you need to.

FIREFLY FLOW

1 Place hands and practice the pattern

- Play a low F with LH finger 1.

- Answer by playing G with RH finger 1 and then B with RH finger 3.

- Play F with LH finger 1 again.

- Now move your RH up one note and play A with RH finger 1 and then C with RH finger 3.

- Keep climbing your RH up the keyboard.

KEEP CLIMBING YOUR RH UP!

2 Play the pattern

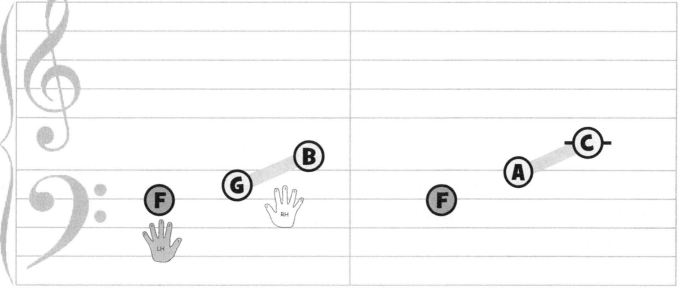

KEEP CLIMBING YOUR RH UP!

WALTZ TIME!

Did you know that you just played a waltz? A waltz is a type of classical dance song that has three beats per measure.

Try playing the waltz above these ways to really make it shine!

Combine the song above with the last song, "Flickering Fireflies."

Add pedal.

FLOW

Play high on the keyboard.

Look up famous waltzes like "Blue Danube" and "The Skater's Waltz."

Get into the flow. Play the song then explore all over with the pattern for 3 minutes.

SUPER CHALLENGE: METEOR SHOWER

I Place hands and practice the pattern

● Play middle C with LH finger 1.

● Place your RH one octave higher, and answer by playing E with RH finger 3 and then C with RH finger 1.

● Play middle C with LH finger 1 again.

● Move your RH down one note, and play D with RH finger 3 and then B with RH finger 1.

● Keep climbing your RH down the keyboard until it meets your left hand.

PLAY THE PATTERN

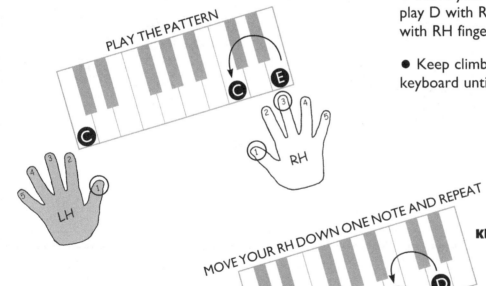

MOVE YOUR RH DOWN ONE NOTE AND REPEAT

KEEP CLIMBING YOUR RH DOWN!

2 Play the pattern

3 Experiment

Can you play like...

1 Fast meteors!	**2** Low, slow meteors!
3 Smooth shooting stars.	**4** Quiet, distant meteors.

Try playing with the pedal!

Super Challenge!

Double up!
Play each pattern twice before moving your RH.
Middle C, E, C,
Middle C, E, C
and so on...

CLIMB DOWN ONE MORE TIME!

QUANTUM QUIZ!

1 **Knowledge.** A third is one step bigger than a _____.

2 **Meteoric Thirds!** Play a third starting on each note below. (For example, for C, you'll play C and E to make a third.)

C

E

B

G

D

A

F

3 **Perform!** Play "Firefly Flow" for family or friends.

 Congrats! You've learned to play thirds and earned more powers! Now let's put your pattern skills to work in your very own concert!

THIRDS   FLOW

Welcome to the Finale Frontier, home of Planet Plunk's biggest, best concert hall.

In this chapter, we'll apply all you've learned about hands, keys and patterns to play some great-sounding songs in your very own finale concert. Then you'll create your very own song!

FIREFLY FANTASIA, MOVEMENT I

In classical music, larger compositions are sometimes divided into sections, called "movements." Here's the first movement of this fantasia!

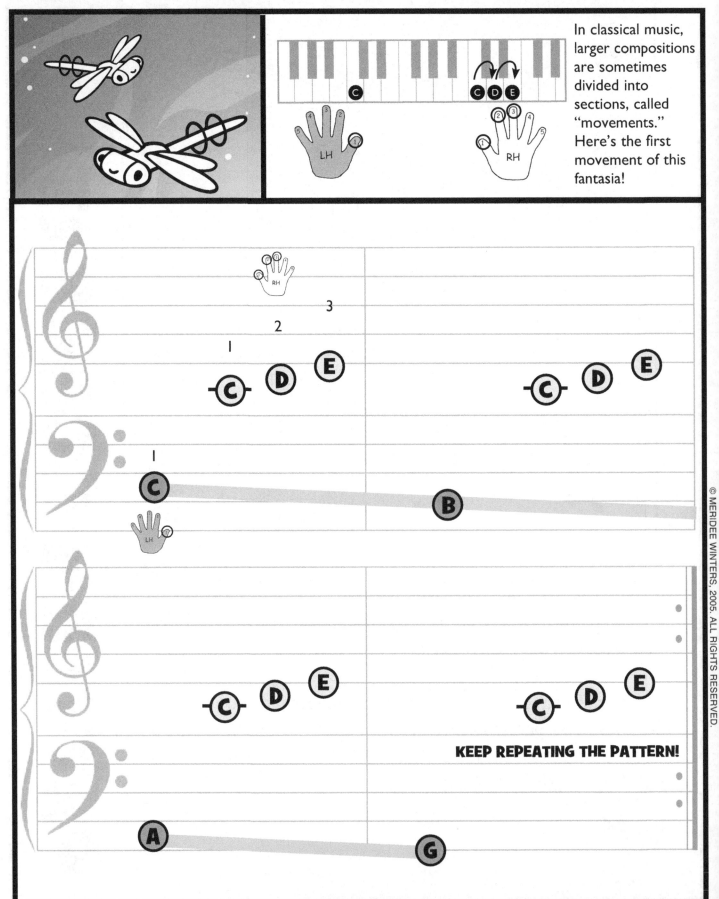

KEEP REPEATING THE PATTERN!

MERIDEE WINTERS SUPER START! MY FIRST PIANO PATTERNS

FIREFLY FANTASIA, MOVEMENT 2

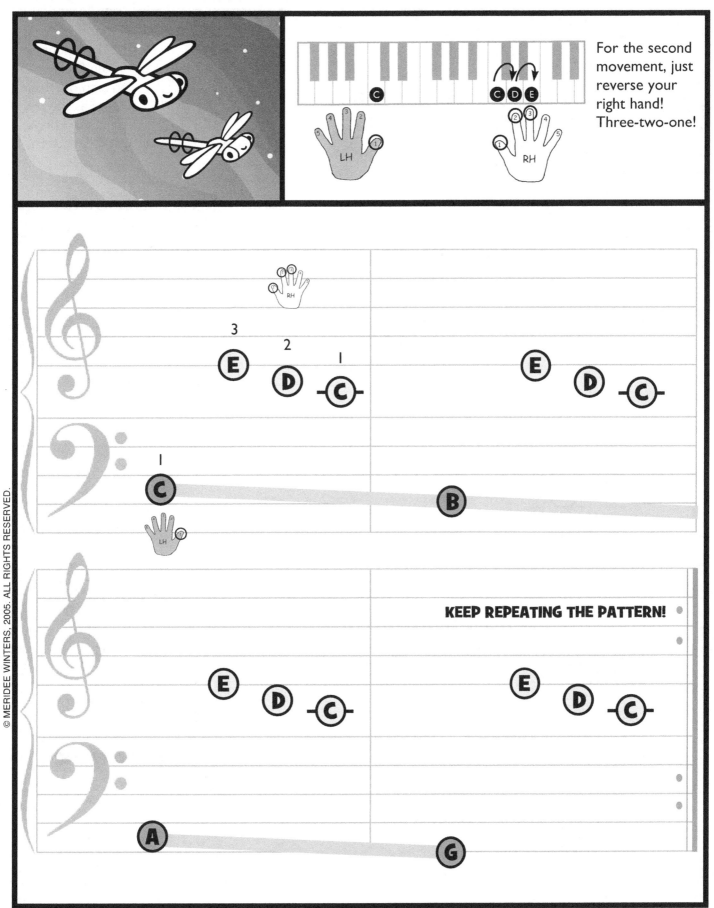

For the second movement, just reverse your right hand! Three-two-one!

KEEP REPEATING THE PATTERN!

FIREFLY FANTASIA, MOVEMENT 3

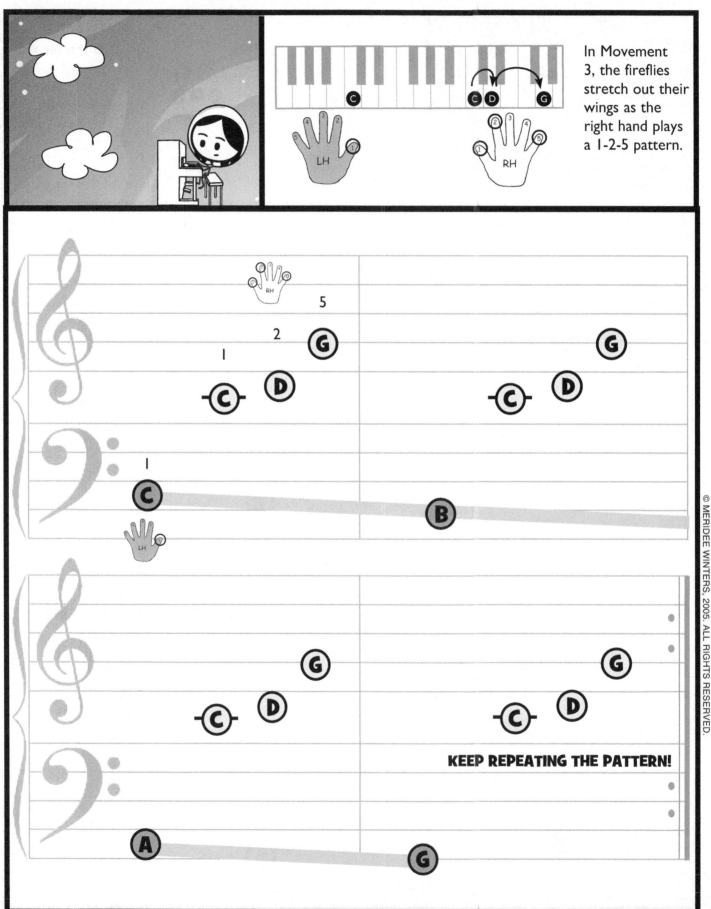

In Movement 3, the fireflies stretch out their wings as the right hand plays a 1-2-5 pattern.

KEEP REPEATING THE PATTERN!

FIREFLY FANTASIA, MOVEMENT 4

Your right hand will now play a pattern starting with your 5 finger. Then you'll get to create your own song!

KEEP REPEATING THE PATTERN!

TITLE:

TITLE:

Draw your own picture to go with the song!

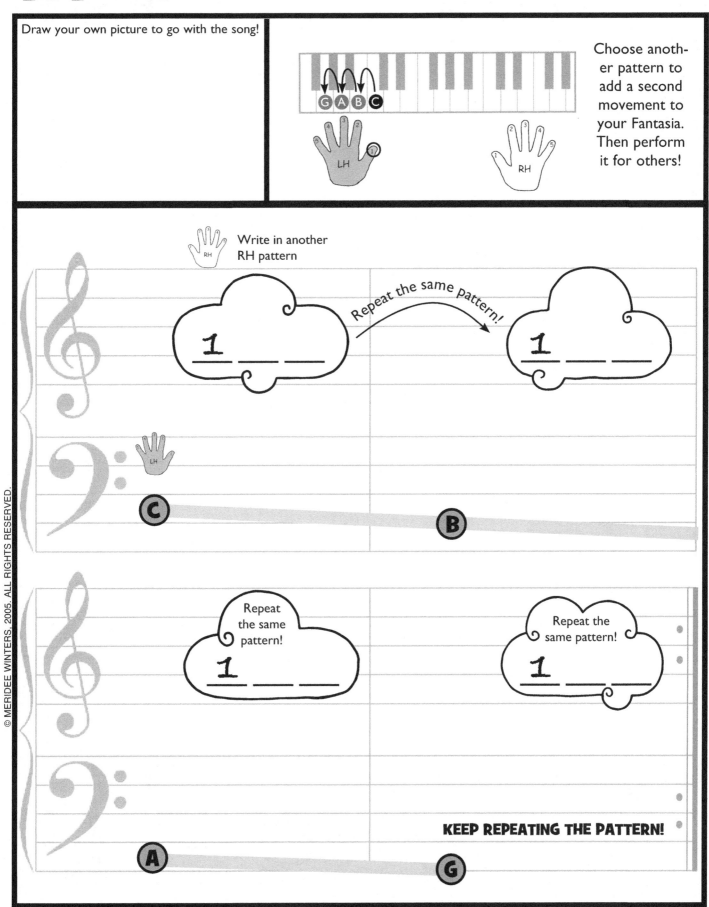

Choose another pattern to add a second movement to your Fantasia. Then perform it for others!

Write in another RH pattern

Repeat the same pattern!

1 ___ ___ ___

1 ___ ___ ___

C ———— B

Repeat the same pattern!

1 ___ ___ ___

Repeat the same pattern!

1 ___ ___ ___

KEEP REPEATING THE PATTERN!

A ———— G

YOUR CONCERT

Write in any notes, a review of your performance, a concert program and more!

What an amazing concert! you've come so far. Just one more challenge awaits: your FINAL TEST!

Chapter 8

FINAL TEST

You've done it! You've learned great songs, gained knowledge and explored Planet Plunk.

BUT... You have one last mission before you can move onto your next great adventure, Chord Quest Book 1!

You'll need to pass a final test. Don't worry, though. You've earned all the powers you need along the way! Also – C.C. Copycat's students will be watching. Now is your chance to show them there's more to music than just copying what others play!

FINAL TEST: PROVE YOUR KNOWLEDGE

1 Knowledge

Fill in the note names on the keyboard

Play a second.

Play a third.

2 Perform

Perform your favorite song from this book. Add dynamics and personality!

Notes on the performance: _____

_____

MERIDEE WINTERS SUPER START! MY FIRST PIANO PATTERNS

FINAL TEST, CONTINUED

 Improvise

Improvise at the piano for at least ONE minute. Explore. Get into the flow.

Notes on your improv: _____

_____

_____

FINAL TEST: ARPEGGIO CHALLENGE

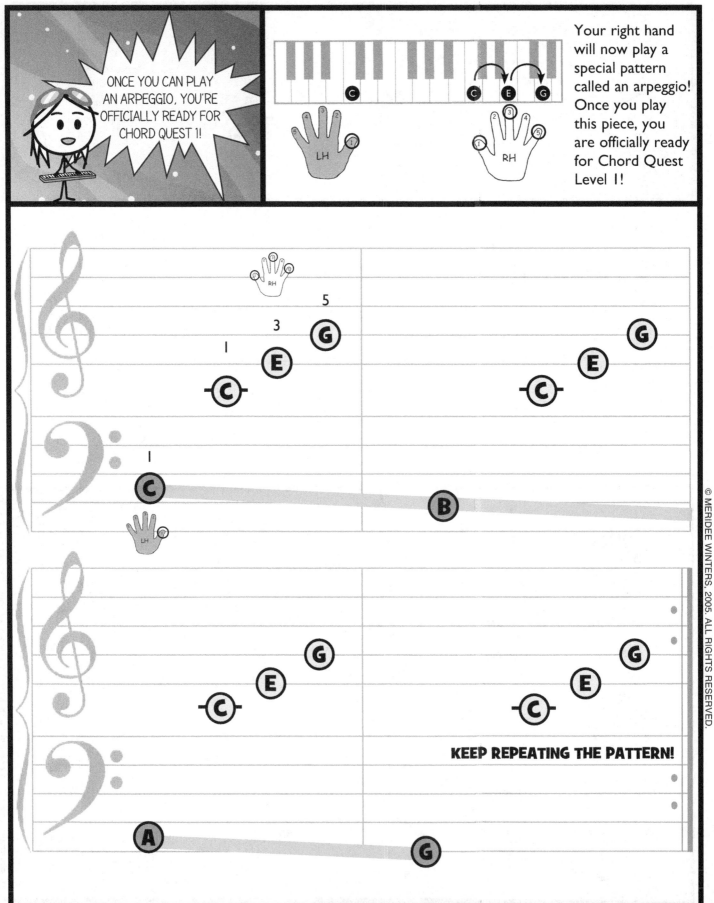

ADD ARTISTRY

Make your arpeggio performance unique by playing these ways.

Play slowly and mysteriously.

Play quietly.

Play quickly and joyfully.

Play high on the keyboard.

Create an ending by playing C arpeggios all the way up the keyboard.

Play loudly.

Pay no attention to this game! Remember: when games are played, learning is delayed!

...DITTO! COME BACK HERE!

Choose your own way to play.

YOU DID IT!

COPYCAT'S STUDENTS NOW UNDERSTAND THE POWER OF CREATIVITY! THEY'RE DONE WITH THEIR COPYCAT LESSONS.

EVEN HER CAT, DITTO, WANTS TO ABANDON HIS "BLAH" WAYS!

NOW YOU CAN KEEP DEFENDING CREATIVITY... IN CHORD QUEST 1!

AWARD

CONGRATULATIONS!

_____

Has successfully completed the
Meridee Winters Super Start! My First Piano Patterns Book
and may now graduate to Meridee Winters Chord Quest Level 1!

Signed _____

Date _____

You did it!
You're ready to try Chord
Quest! Check out the next
few pages for a sneak peek
from that book!

Let's surf
on over to
Chord Quest!

ARPEGGIOS

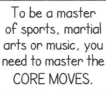

To be a master of sports, martial arts or music, you need to master the CORE MOVES.

In karate, you learn center punch and front kick. In basketball you learn dribbling and shooting. In space training, you simulate missions.

In music, the core power moves are CHORDS and ARPEGGIOS. They are used by millions of musicians every day.

CHORDS

ARPEGGIOS

In Chord Quest Level 1, you'll learn about chords, arpeggios and so much more!

Let's take a sneak peek and learn more about arpeggios!

Now that you've finished "Super Start! My First Piano Patterns," you're ready to move to Meridee's "Chord Quest Powerful Piano Lessons" Series!

This chapter is a top secret sneak peek at Chord Quest Level 1. You just played an arpeggio in your Super Start test - now you'll get to hear it with one of the most famous chord progressions of all time.

Let's take a look at Chord Quest Level 1!

CHORD SNEAK PEEK QUEST

CHORD QUEST SNEAK PEEK

TWO-HANDED ARPEGGIOS

You've already played arpeggios.
Let's try it with both hands!

PLACE HANDS...

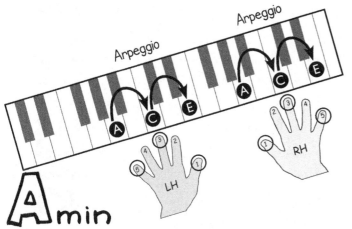

- Place your left hand pinky on the A below middle C and your right hand thumb on the next A.
- Play an A minor arpeggio with your left hand by playing the notes shown on the diagram.
- Answer with an A minor arpeggio in your right hand.
- Move both hands down one note to G position and repeat the pattern.
- Move to F and repeat.
- Move to E and repeat.

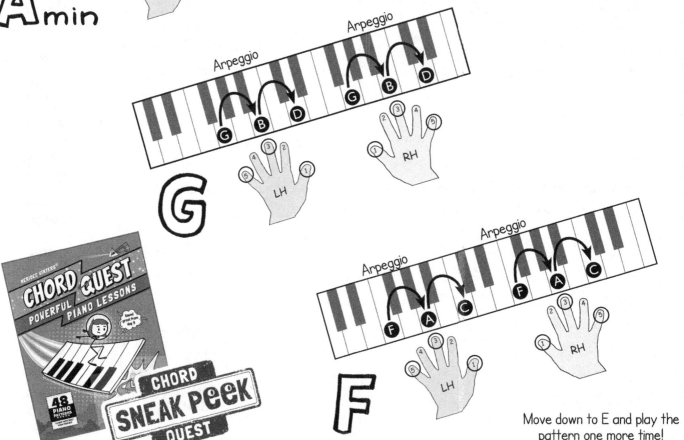

Move down to E and play the pattern one more time!

WHAT IS A CHORD PROGRESSION?

To build a progression, put chords or arpeggios into different orders.

It's called a chord progression even when it's played with arpeggios. You'll learn chords in Chapter 3 of Chord Quest Level 1!

This progression is famous, and has been used in Spanish and classical music for hundreds of years.

8 MAGNETIC MALAGUENA

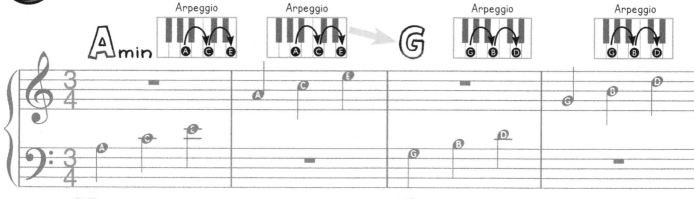

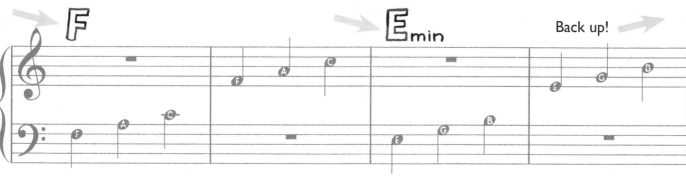

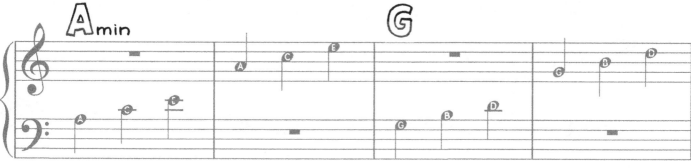

THE MERIDEE WINTERS MUSIC METHOD
☆ Sparking brilliance with patterns, chords and games ☆

Want to supercharge your progress with your instrument or find a tool to help you create music?

Find Meridee's globally-popular, trailblazing instructional books, innovative music games, online lesson info and more at merideewintersmusicmethod.com – or find us on Amazon.com!

YOUR NEXT QUEST!

EVIL VILLAINS

CHORD QUEST SERIES

Our brains are wired to excel at patterns. Finally, a kid's music book that teaches that way. (And sure has fun doing it.)

What do you get when you take the great content and innovative teaching style from *Chord Crash Course*, but design and pace it for school aged kids? The *Chord Quest Powerful Piano Lessons* Series! Like its older counterpart, *Chord Quest* uses the power of patterns and shapes to have students playing great-sounding music from the very first lesson — without reading music. **Each book is its own quest where students learn universal patterns, earn powers and defeat villains like the Baron von Boring!**

PORTALS & POWERS

EXPLORE THE WORLD

MERIDEE WINTERS EASY PIANO SONGS FOR KIDS

Meridee Winters Easy Piano Songs for Kids: The Ultimate Collection of Beginner Classics is a carefully curated collection of over 70 amazing songs from around the world.

Designed so that even beginners can play great-sounding songs (without the filler), these thoughtful arrangements are destined to be loved, memorized and performed. With primer level and level 1 songs, "Meridee Winters Easy Piano Songs for Kids" is the perfect companion to the Super Start and Chord Quest Series, or a great standalone repertoire collection!

Meridee Winters Music Method ☆ merideewintersmusicmethod.com

Made in the USA
Coppell, TX
29 January 2022

72601969R00050